FOREST ANIMALS

BENDON®
Publishing International, Inc.

© 2013
Ashland, OH 44805
www.bendonpub.com

all images © Dreamstime, iStockPhoto LP and Shutterstock, Inc.

FOREST ANIMALS

There are many forest animals.

Some are active in the day and some prefer the night.

BLUE JAY

Birds fly around the forest all day long.

The blue jay squawks its name, "jay, jay, jay".

Each bird has a different song.

SQUIRREL

Squirrels have long **furry tails** and hunt for **nuts** to eat.

Squirrels live in the **forest**, too.

They chatter with each other all day long.

DEER

The mother deer is called a doe.

She keeps her baby close to her. Her baby is called a fawn.

It has white spots so it can hide easily in the bushes.

The father deer is called a stag. He has antlers on his head.

RABBiT

The rabbits in the forest live in homes underground.

They hop around looking for grass and leaves to nibble.

CHIPMUNK

A little chipmunk sits in the sun.

It will soon look for nuts to eat.

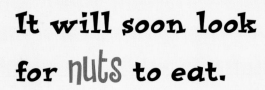

Some of the nuts it eats now.

Others it hides for Later.

SNAKE

A snake comes out of its hole in the ground and finds a nice **sunny** place to stop and rest.

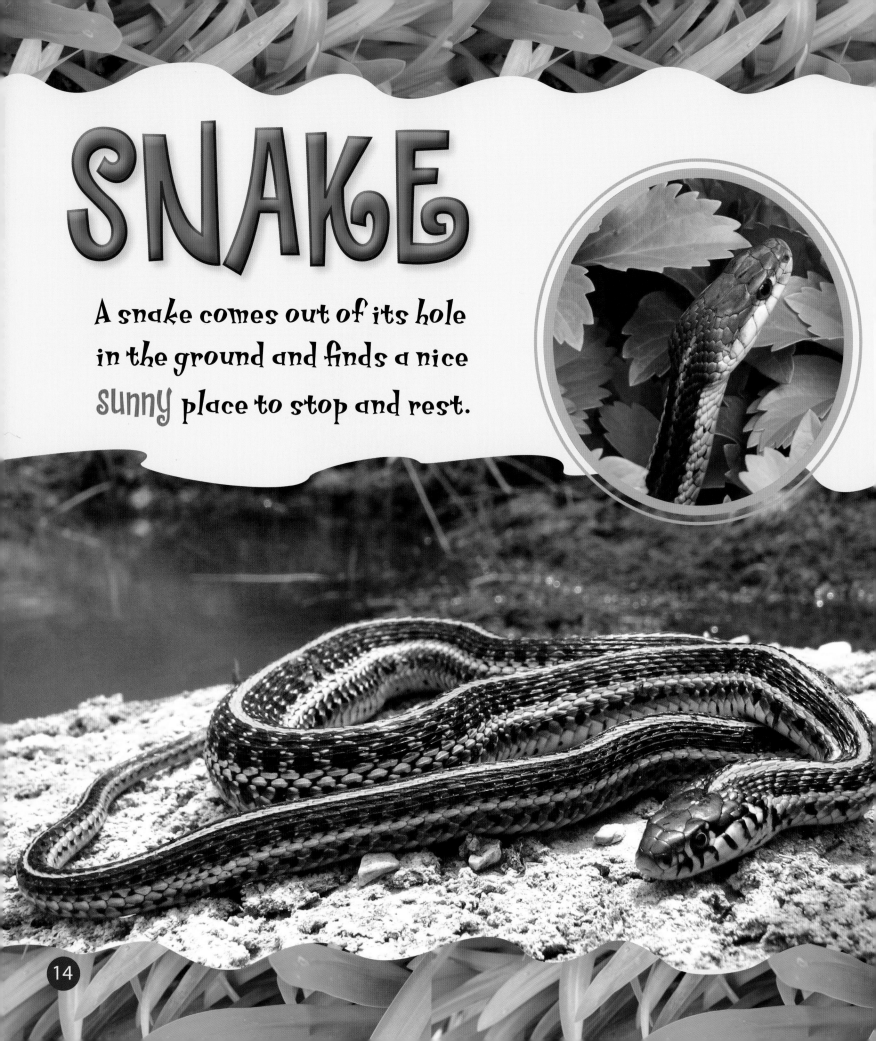

As it grows, a snake will shed its old skin and leave it behind on the ground.

OWL

At **night**, the owl comes out of the tree to look for food.

It flies so quietly it can sneak up on the tiny animals on the ground.

RACCOON

Raccoons have a face that looks like they are wearing a **mask**.

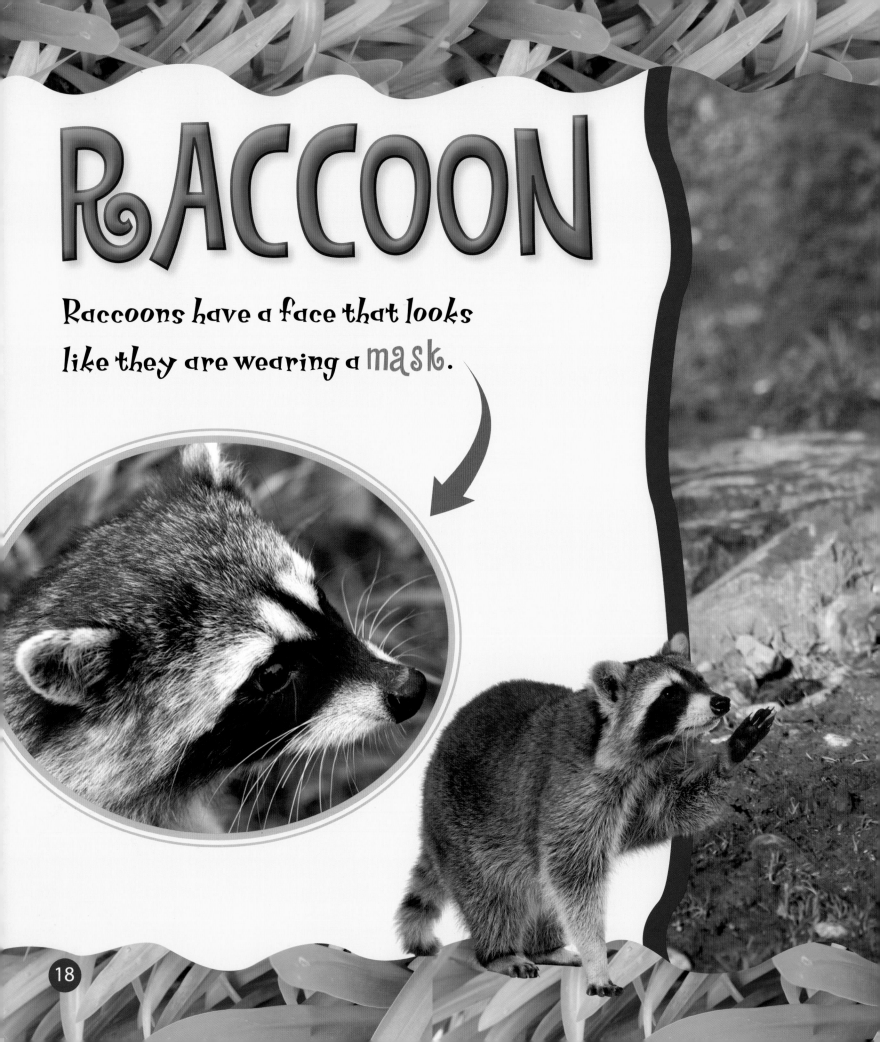

Raccoons look for food around the forest after dark along with another forest creature with a particularly bad odor.

Can you guess which animal that is?

SKUNK

That's right!

It is a skunk!

Skunks don't spray their **stinky** scent unless they are frightened.

So it is best to stay far away from a skunk if you see one while walking in the **forest**.

QUESTIONS

1. Can you name 2 different kinds of birds?

2. Where do squirrels build their homes?

3. What is a mother deer called?

4. What is a father deer called?

5. What is a baby deer called?

6. What does a chipmunk do with the nuts it finds?

7. Can you name an animal that sleeps during the day and hunts at night?

8. Where do owls live?

9. What does a raccoon's face look like?

ACTIVITIES

1 Look around your backyard, neighborhood, or local nature trail. Count how many birds you see. What other animals do you see?

_____

2 Would a skunk make a good pet? Write the reasons below.

_____

_____

3 Make up your own forest animal. Draw it here!

4 If you could be any kind of forest animal, what would it be? Write your answer below.

_____